D0877614

...votions de la Ste vierge, ils se mettront de ses confrair...
t puis ils n'en pratiquent point les regles avec fid...
ils changent comme la lune et Marie les met sou...
pieds avec eux sans parcequ'ils sont changeants et
indignes d'être comptez parmi les serviteurs de cette...
fidele qui ont la fidelité et la constance pour part...
Vaut mieux ne pas se charger de tant de prieres, et...
pratiques de devotion et en faire peu avec amour e...
fidelité malgré le monde le diable et la chair.
Il y a encore de faux devots a la ste vierge qui son...
es devots hyppocrites qui couvrent leurs pechez, et le...
acumaires habituelles sous le manteau de cette vierge f...
ffin de passer aux yeux des hommes pour ce qu'ils ne...
as; il y a encore des devots interessez qui ne recourent...
se la vierge que pour gagner quelque procez pou...
viter quelque peril, pour guerir d'une maladie ou...
quelqu'autre besoin de cette sorte, sans quoi ils l'oubli...
les uns et les autres sont de faux devots qui ne son...
point de mises devant Dieu ni sa ste mere.
Prenons donc bien garde d'être du nombre des deu...

THE
SECRET
OF
MARY

CONCERNING SLAVERY
TO THE HOLY VIRGIN

ST. LOUIS DE MONTFORT

MONTFORT PUBLICATIONS

Ad Jesum per Mariam

Nihil Obstat
THOMAS W. SMIDDY, S.T.L.

Imprimatur
†THOMAS EDMUND MOLLOY, S.T.D.
Bishop of Brooklyn
4 June 1947

Imprimi Potest
A. JOSSELIN, S.M.M.,
Superior GeneMONTral

MontfortPublications.com

Revised Edition
First Printing 2016

MONTFORTPUBLICATIONS
26 South Saxon Ave.
Bay Shore, NY 11706

CONTENTS

An Introduction and Overview

THE SECRET OF MARY

Concerning Slavery to the Holy Virgin

Abridged and adapted from the article *Secret of Mary* by Fr. Alphonse Bossard, SMM,
that is included in *Jesus Living in Mary: A Handbook of Montfort Spirituality*,

Montfort Publications (1994).

1. THE TEXT AND ITS HISTORY

A. State of the text and its editions

We do not have Fr. de Montfort's original manuscript. Its text has come to us by way of two copies, one preserved in the archives of the Company of Mary, the other in the archives of the Daughters of Wisdom. The few variant readings that they contain in no way affect the essentials of the content.

The copy used in the official edition of St. Louis de Montfort's collected works (hereafter referred to as OC) bears the following heading: "Copy of a manuscript that the late Father de Montfort had written by hand and sent to a person of piety." Sister Florence, a Daughter of Wisdom who wrote a valuable chronicle (which ends in 1761), observes: "By the same channel we received this admirable letter on the devotion of the Holy Slavery of Jesus in Mary, which Father de Montfort wrote to a religious Sister of Nantes. There were three prayers that were later placed at the end of the letter: one addressed to Jesus, another for those preaching the Holy Slavery,

[1] *Chroniques de Soeur Florence (Chronicals of Sister Florence),* 95.

and the third entitled by the man of God 'Multiplication of the Philosophers' Stone, or Cultivation of the Tree of Life.'"[1] This "same channel" of which Sister Florence speaks "is doubtless Joseau and Brother Jacques. A companion of Fr. de Montfort since 1714, Brother Jacques settled at Saint-Laurent-sur-Sèvre in 1716 and became friendly with a young man named Joseau, to whom he gave the writings of Father de Montfort to be copied" (OC, 440).

In any event, the copy dates from the first half of the eighteenth century; and despite the loss of the original manuscript, the attribution of the text to St. Louis Marie de Montfort is beyond all doubt. Indeed, the content and style alone would be signature enough.

While fragments of the text are found in various biographies of Father de Montfort, only in 1868 did a first edition make its appearance. It was not until the manuscript of St. Louis de Montfort's masterwork, *The Treatise upon True Devotion to the Holy Virgin* (hereafter referred to as TD) was rediscovered, published, and met with prompt success that the interest and value of *The Secret of Mary* came to light. In 1898 Father Lhoumeau published the text almost in its entirety; the only omissions are of certain pas-

sages bearing on the wearing of little chains as a sign of the Consecration of the slaves of Jesus in Mary.[2] The Lhoumeau edition itself contains a certain number of explanatory notes. It is to Father Huré that we owe the first *"type"* edition, that is, one entirely conformed to the manuscript, "furnished with an 'analytical division' whose elements, placed at each important break in the text, briefly summarize the context of the text they precede" (preface, p. iv). Furthermore, marginal numerals were used, "which will henceforward ensure the uniformity of references, despite the diversity of editions" (ibid., p. v).

The editors of official edition of St. Louis de Montfort's collected works, while retaining the marginal numbering introduced by Father Huré, have undertaken a painstakingly minute revision of the text, which has resulted in "the correction of certain textual mistakes found in the previous editions" (OC, 441).

It is difficult to give the exact number of editions of The Secret of Mary; a very reasonable estimate of 350 editions might be suggested.

[2] This "omission" is explained by criticisms that the wearing of this symbol could have occasioned. Certain abuses provoked by the wearing of these little chains had led the Holy See, at the end of the eighteenth century, to proscribe their usage and to condemn certain books of particular confraternities. While aimed only at the abuses, these condemnations nevertheless cast a pall over this practice. The prudence of the editors of SM is understandable.

B. Literary genre and addressee(s)

The text is presented in the form of a *"letter,"* in which the author addresses a *"soul"* - someone whom Saint Louis Marie seeks to convince of the excellence of the spiritual way he proclaims. The heading to which we have referred ("Copy of a manuscript that the late Father de Montfort had written by hand and sent to a person of piety"), along with Sister Florence's declaration about "this admirable letter, which Monsieur de Montfort wrote to a religious Sister of Nantes on the devotion of Holy Slavery of Jesus in Mary," suggests that the addressee was a particular individual.

None of the several hypotheses that have been advanced for identifying this individual is particularly compelling. However, this would not seem to be a matter of the first importance. The fact that St. Louis Marie sent his *"letter"* to this or that "person of piety" rather than to another changes little when it comes to an understanding of the text. Indeed, while the tone Fr. de Montfort employs is personal (as is also the tone in a number of passages of his other writings), the text itself teaches us next to nothing about the precise person to whom it is addressed - nei-

ther the person's state, milieu, character, current difficulties, or the like - unless we think we find a personal indication in the reference in SM 2 to what little time is at the reader's disposition, but this scarcely tells us much about the individual. The only conclusion we can draw about the addressee is that she (the soul) is a person of good will and capable of understanding the message being communicated. Otherwise, apart from the doctrinal knowledge and profound spiritual experience to which the text testifies, St. Louis Marie tells us nothing about the precise individual. If this is a letter, it is very different from his existing personal letters. Were it not for the remarks that we have indicated, we could imagine a sort of "circular letter," intended for a number of persons and yet sent to a particular individual, of whom Fr. de Montfort would have thought more particularly as he was writing it.

A personal style, in which the author addresses himself directly to his reader, could be regarded as a literary device altogether appropriate for a work of general interest. And in the case of *The Secret of Mary*, it is scarcely artificial. Apart from certain expressions or constructions pointing to a cultural milieu that obviously is no longer the same for us today, there is no reason why

today's reader should not understand himself or herself directly and personally addressed by Fr. de Montfort. The style endows the text with a freshness and simplicity that are not least among its values.

C. Title

We owe the title of the work not to St. Louis Marie but to the first publishers, and it is an appropriate one. First, Fr. de Montfort is fond of the popular word "secret." Second, in SM 20, he speaks of a *"secret of Mary"*: *"Happy, indeed sublimely happy, is the person to whom the Holy Spirit reveals the secret of Mary, thus imparting to him true knowledge of her. Happy the person to whom the Holy Spirit opens this enclosed garden for him to enter, and to whom the Holy Spirit gives access to this sealed fountain where he can draw water and drink deep draughts of the living waters of grace"* (SM 20). The expression "secret" has a strong, complex meaning for him. In herself, Mary is a secret. That is, she is hidden (cf. TD 2–13), too beautiful, too rich, too great, too filled by God for us to be able to understand her. Only the Holy Spirit can give us access to her wealth, since the Holy Spirit is the author of that wealth.

Another meaning of the word "secret" for Fr. de Montfort is that Mary can enable us to enter into the very mystery of God. She is the *"marvelous means"* given to us by God to permit us to arrive at holiness, which is union with Jesus Christ. St. Louis Marie calls for an implementation, a life experience of *"drawing"* on Mary and of *"drinking deep draughts of the living waters of grace."*

Finally, for Fr. de Montfort, what he calls the *"perfect practice of the true devotion,"* by which we strive to make all possible room for Mary in our life in order to reach Jesus and be united with him, is a *"secret of holiness"* (H 77:19), *"his"* secret. For it is a means, according to him the best means, to arrive at the goal the Lord proposes us. It is this secret that he seeks to reveal to his reader: *"Here is a secret, chosen soul, which the most High God taught me"* (SM 1). This secret is rooted in Mary. Since Fr. de Montfort is convinced that it is his mission to make known her place in the divine plan, the title, *Secret of Mary,* is well chosen.

II. ANALYSIS

The manuscript used by the editors of official edition of St. Louis de Montfort's collected works is a continuous text, with only an occasional "1" or "2" to indicate items in a list. It is thanks to internal criticism, then, that it has been possible to propose divisions. While the marginal numerals added by the *type* edition of 1926 have been retained by the editors, the latter have rather thoroughly recast the divisions and the wording of their headings. They have been concerned to show a kind of parallelism between the structure of *The Secret of Mary* and that of *The Treatise upon True Devotion to the Holy Virgin*. The outline proposed is as follows:

Author's Introduction (1–2)

I. Necessity of Having a True Devotion to Mary (3–23)

> **A.** The grace of God is absolutely necessary (3–5)
> **B.** To find the grace of God, we must discover Mary (6–22)
> **C.** A true devotion to the Blessed Virgin is indispensable (23)

2. How to cultivate it (71–77)

3. Its lasting fruit: Jesus Christ (78)

One need only glance at the outline of TD in OC to observe that with a certain flexibility—TD being notably more developed—the basic structure is the same: it is the same spiritual way or path, founded on the same profound considerations.

III. CONTRIBUTIONS OF THE SECRET OF MARY

A. THE FIRST PART

1. Introduction

"*Here is a secret, chosen soul, which the most High God taught me and which I have not found in any book, ancient or modern*" (SM 1). St. Louis Marie is making three assertions here. First, he states that he is about to reveal a secret, which here means a hidden reality that is at the same time an exceptional means to the attainment of a goal (in this case, holiness, the perfection of the Christian life). Next, he states that he has himself received this secret directly from the Most High. St. Louis de Montfort is aware of the grace that he has obtained of knowing Mary and her mission and of taking her into his life "to himself," like John the Apostle. We must take this statement seriously, for it means that we ourselves shall be able to attain to this knowledge of Mary only through grace. Finally, Fr. de Montfort tells us straight out that he has not found this secret *"in any book, ancient or modern"* (SM 1). Now, in-

asmuch as he asserts elsewhere that the "devotion" constituting his secret is old, has been approved by the Holy See, and has been practiced by *"many saints and illustrious people"* (SM 42; cf. TD 18, 159), how are we to reconcile these seemingly so different assertions?

While St. Louis de Montfort has indeed found the Holy Slavery of the Mother of God in various authors (especially in the works of Henri Boudon), as well as various formulas of Consecration, the fact remains that it is he who has been able to bestow upon this form of Marian devotion an original, new expression. In a certain sense, he has transformed it, and he has not found it in books such as he expounds it and proposes it. For that matter, inasmuch as it is question of a "secret" that can acquire its whole meaning only for one *who lives it by putting it in practice*, books do not suffice for its discovery: *"This secret becomes great only insofar as a soul makes use of it. . . . As you go on using this secret in the ordinary actions of your life, you will come to understand its value and its excellent quality"* (SM 1).

2. Goal of our life and means of attaining it

The argumentation employed by Fr. de Montfort for the purpose of demonstrating that Mary is necessary for us is, in its basic elements, the same in *The Secret of Mary* and *The Treatise upon True Devotion to the Holy Virgin*. More briefly in *The Secret of Mary*, it begins by placing before us, with theological precision, the goal of our life: *"Chosen soul, living image of God and redeemed by the precious blood of Jesus Christ, God wants you to become holy like him in this life and glorious like him in the next"* (SM 3). What we are -- the image of God by creation and saved, redeemed by Christ -- just by itself explains that we do not belong to ourselves and that we receive the goal of our life from the One from whom we have our life and our salvation. What God wants for us is simply that we should share in the divine holiness here below in order to share in the divine glory in the next world. Thus, right from the outset, and in few words, the whole love of God is set before our eyes. But it follows that we must respond to it.

"It is certain that growth in the holiness of God is your vocation." There is no point in looking elsewhere. Our calling does not depend on us but on God's love for us. That marks a path for us upon

which we ought to set out without any reservations: *"All your thoughts, words, actions, everything you suffer or undertake must lead you towards that end. Otherwise you are resisting God in not doing the work for which he created you and for which he is even now keeping you in being"* (SM 3). How are we to find this grace? In finding Mary: *"It all comes to this, then. We must discover a simple means to obtain from God the grace needed to become holy. It is precisely this I wish to teach you. My contention is that you must first discover Mary if you would obtain this grace from God"* (SM 6). Fr. de Montfort then sets forth, much more briefly than in *The Treatise upon True Devotion to the Holy Virgin*, the arguments upon which his conviction is based (SM 7–23).

3. "Necessity" of Mary

SM 24, which concludes this part, poses a minor problem of interpretation. *"The difficulty, then, is how to arrive at the true knowledge of the most holy Virgin and so find grace in abundance through her. God as the absolute Master, can give directly what he ordinarily dispenses only through Mary, and it would be rash to deny that he sometimes does so. However, St. Thomas assures*

us that, following the order established by his divine Wisdom, God ordinarily imparts his graces to men through Mary. Therefore, if we wish to go to him, seeking union with him, we must use the same means which he used in coming down from heaven to assume our human nature and to impart his graces to us. That means was a complete dependence on Mary his Mother, which is true devotion to her" (SM 24).

At one moment in the relatively recent past, when Mariologists were deeply concerned with debating the question of the "universal mediation of Mary," the interpretation of this text of Fr. de Montfort acquired a particular importance. Some Mariologists had difficulty in accepting from St. Louis de Montfort what seemed to them to be a distortion of the principle of the universal mediation.

Very simply, St. Louis Marie's concern is different from that of a university professor; he is a preacher of parish missions. He knows, however, that he must take certain precautions in order to found his conclusions solidly and not leave his flank open to criticisms of "exaggerations" in his conceptualization of Mary's mission and the practice of the devotion to her that he heralds.

St. Louis de Montfort, good theologian that

he is, makes a distinction. He knows perfectly well that God is *"absolute Master"* (SM 23) and that *"this great Lord, who is ever independent and self-sufficient, never had and does not now have any absolute need of the Blessed Virgin for the accomplishment of his will and the manifestation of his glory. To do all things he has only to will them"* (TD 14). God alone can determine, in all Wisdom and Love, what is to be accomplished in the divine plan and the ways to accomplish it. If Mary is "necessary," it is because God wills her to be necessary, and she is necessary to the extent that God wills it.

It is possible, therefore, and very useful to seek out the pathways that the Lord has actually chosen in order to come to us, and the ways that same Lord asks us to take in order to go to God. But what God's ordinary manner of acting teaches us is that He wishes to use Mary in the communication and obtaining of grace. Fr. de Montfort has been showing this in the preceding numbers, and that is what is important for him. Who could decree that God, in the absolute divine power, might not do otherwise or even that God does not at times actually do so? Does He? For St. Louis de Montfort, the question is and remains purely hypothetical, and he has no need of burdening himself with it. Having taken all necessary pre-

cautions lest he be accused of unduly encroaching upon the mystery of God or of proposing a false notion of the person of Mary and her mission, he simply pursues his exposition. We then encounter Fr. de Montfort's profound vision of the Incarnation. In it he perceives the manner of God's action. He sees everything as flowing from this mysterious source, for Mary and for us. *"If we wish to go to him, seeking union with him, we must use the same means which he used in coming down"* to us.

B. THE SECOND PART:
The exposition on "what perfect devotion to Mary consists in"

After having briefly indicated that there are *"several true devotions to our Lady,"* Fr. de Montfort arrives at the one dearest to his heart: the perfect practice of true devotion. In The *Treatise upon True Devotion to the Holy Virgin*, St. Louis de Montfort likewise, and in a much more developed fashion, presents his teaching on the perfect devotion to Our Lady. It is important, therefore, to consider the teaching set forth by Fr. de Montfort in both of these works together, noting both the strong similarities of content and the important differences in expression between

them, in order to fully appreciate the breadth and depth of his treatment of the perfect devotion of Holy Slavery to Jesus living in Mary as well as the particular richness to be found in a close reading of *The Secret of Mary.*

1. What this "devotion" consists in

The definition that St. Louis Marie gives of his perfect practice of the true devotion is, in a way, more synthetic and more precise than the one we find in TD: *"Chosen soul, this devotion consists in surrendering oneself in the manner of a slave to Mary, and to Jesus through her, and then performing all our actions with Mary, in Mary, through Mary, and for Mary"* (SM 28). The two elements that constitute the spiritual path proposed by Fr. de Montfort are clearly defined and intertwined: the total Consecration (or total gift) of oneself to Jesus through Mary; and what he calls in TD the *"interior practices"* (TD 257) and in SM 60 simply the *"interior practice."* He reiterates the principle that this interior practice belongs to the essence of the spiritual way in question: *"I have already said that this devotion consists in performing all our actions with Mary, in Mary, through Mary, and for Mary"* (SM 43). While it is not difficult to draw

this conclusion on the basis of the presentation in TD, it must be acknowledged that on this so important point, SM furnishes a clearer and more explicit formulation.

2. The manner in which the interior practice is presented

The interior practice is presented with several variants in SM and TD: *"Performing all our actions with Mary, in Mary, through Mary, and for Mary"* (SM 43); *"Doing everything through Mary, with Mary, in Mary and for Mary, in order to do it more perfectly **through** Jesus, **with** Jesus, **in** Jesus and **for** Jesus"* (TD 257).

A first difference strikes the reader at once: the order of the prepositions is not the same. Ultimately, this is not very important in and of itself. A closer examination reveals that not quite the same things are said by way of explanation of the prepositions "through" and "with." In SM 45, to act *"with Mary"* means that Mary is taken *"as the accomplished model for all we have to do."* In TD 260, the same idea is expressed in more developed fashion: *"We must look upon Mary, although a simple human being, as the perfect model of every virtue and perfection, fashioned by the Holy Spirit for us to*

imitate, as far as our limited capacity allows." But next Montfort will state in SM under *"with Mary"* what he has developed in TD under *"for Mary"*: that we must renounce ourselves in order to commit ourselves to Mary.

Further, the explanation of *"for Mary"* in SM is very brief: *"We must never go to our Lord except through Mary, using her intercession and good standing with him. We must never be without her when praying to Jesus"* (SM 48). This idea is a familiar one in Montfort (cf., e.g., TD 142–43), and he develops it in very rich fashion in TD 258 in order to explain *"through Mary"*: it is a matter of obeying Mary *"always and being led in all things by her spirit, which is the Holy Spirit of God."* We find something of the kind in SM 55: *"This devotion faithfully practiced produces countless happy effects in the soul. The most important of them is that it establishes, even here on earth, Mary's life in the soul, so that it is no longer the soul that lives, but Mary who lives in it. In a manner of speaking, Mary's soul becomes identified with the soul of her servant."*

Thus, *"in Mary"* is presented somewhat differently. In SM: *"We must gradually acquire the habit of recollecting ourselves interiorly and so form within us an idea or a spiritual image of Mary. She must become, as it were, an Oratory for the soul*

where we offer up our prayers to God without fear of being ignored. She will be as a Tower of David for us where we can seek safety from all our enemies. She will be a burning lamp lighting up our inmost soul and inflaming us with love for God. She will be a sacred place of repose where we can contemplate God in her company. Finally, Mary will be the only means we will use in going to God, and she will become our intercessor for everything we need. When we pray we will pray in Mary. When we receive Jesus in Holy Communion we will place him in Mary for him to take his delight in her. If we do anything at all, it will be in Mary, and in this way Mary will help us to forget self everywhere and in all things" (SM 47).

In TD 261–64, not altogether the same things are said about *"in Mary."* In SM, it is a question, first, of a certain activity on the part of anyone who seeks to live *"in Mary."* It is up to that individual to form, within himself or herself, a little *"idea or a spiritual image"* of Mary, with all of the consequences and advantages that might accrue. In TD, Montfort begins by describing the splendor of Mary, that *"true earthly paradise of the new Adam"* (TD 261), a splendor that the Holy Spirit was at pains to describe (TD 262); and it is this Spirit alone Who, by a *"special grace,"* can grant *"the unfortunate children of Adam and Eve,*

driven from the earthly paradise," access to this new paradise (TD 263). True, Montfort adds that this grace is to be *"obtained by our fidelity"* (TD 263). The effects described in TD 264 in no way contradict what is said in SM. It is only that they tend to be different, including the last, which reiterates an idea that is of the utmost importance for Montfort: we ought to be *"delighted to remain in Mary,"* in order that *"we may be formed in our Lord and our Lord formed in us"* (TD 264).

A second difference may be noted. While in TD the Christological finality of the interior practice is explicitly and strongly maintained, that finality does not appear in the same way in SM. A closer examination, however, reveals that this essential reference to Christ is actually present, first, in the act of total bestowal of self *"to Mary, and to Jesus through her"* (SM 28), and, next, when there is question of the "spirit" of this devotion, *"which requires an interior dependence on Mary, and effectively becoming her slave and the slave of Jesus through her"* (SM 44).

What are we to conclude from these variants in the two writings? Perhaps simply that we should not adopt hidebound formulas, interesting and expressive as they may be, but ought to undertake to discover their spirit. And from this

viewpoint, the differences we find in SM and TD only underscore the wide-ranging wealth of these formulas. Instead of seeking to discover contradictions in them, we should do better to see their complementarity.

C. THE TWO FINAL PRAYERS AND THE TREE OF LIFE

1. Prayer to Jesus

This is a prayer of thanksgiving to Jesus: *"Most loving Jesus, permit me to express my heartfelt gratitude to you for your kindness in giving me to your holy Mother through the devotion of holy slavery"* (SM 66). After a mention of the benefits of belonging to Mary comes a little development that is very interesting because it forcefully asserts that it is the desire of Jesus himself that we give ourselves utterly to his Mother and because it refers to the example of John at the foot of the Cross: *"Like St. John the Evangelist at the foot of the Cross, I have taken her times without number as my total good and as often have I given myself to her. But if I have not done so as perfectly as you, dear Jesus, would wish, I now do so according to your desire. If you still see in my soul or body anything that does*

not belong to this noble Queen, please pluck it out and cast it far from me, because anything of mine which does not belong to Mary is unworthy of you." (SM 66).

This text is important for grasping the spirit that is at the heart of the Total Consecration and the life that ought to follow from it: Mary is a gift that Jesus himself has given to us (hence the reference to John), and the only way to thank him for it is to make place for Mary in our life, as Jesus desires. Furthermore, if we are able to give ourselves utterly to Mary, is it not because Jesus gives us the grace to do so?

The prayer ends with an appeal to the Holy Spirit, whose association with Mary is appropriately recalled: *"Holy Spirit, grant me all these graces. Implant in my soul the tree of true life, which is Mary. Foster it and cultivate it so that it grows and blossoms and brings forth the fruit of life in abundance"* (SM 67). To this purpose, Fr. de Montfort asks the Spirit to give him *"a great love and a longing for Mary, your exalted spouse. Give me a great trust in her maternal heart and a continuous access to her compassion, so that with her you may truly form Jesus, great and powerful, in me until I attain the fullness of his perfect age"* (SM 67). These last words plainly refer to the essential goal of the way

proposed by St. Louis de Montfort as an authentic and complete spirituality to attain the perfect age of Christ. They also refer to the primary mission of Mary, in her association with the Spirit, to form Jesus Christ in us.

2. *Prayer to Mary for use by her faithful slaves of love*

The prayer that follows begins with a salutation to Mary very much like the one that we find in the prayer at the end of *The Little Crown* (cf. MP 13), with an added statement: *"You are all mine through God's mercy, but I am all yours by justice"* (SM 68). This assertion sheds new light on the relationship of reciprocal belonging between Mary and each person. Mary belongs to us "by mercy," while we belong to her "by justice"-- by reason of all that she has done for us.

Quite naturally, this leads the person uttering the prayer to a renewal of Consecration: *"I am all yours by justice. Yet I do not belong sufficiently to you, and so once again, as a slave who always belongs to his master, I give myself wholly to you, reserving nothing for myself or for others"* (SM 68). The mention of Jesus, to whom this Consecration is ultimately directed, comes later: *"Finally, most dearly beloved Mother, grant, if it be possible, that I may*

have no other spirit but yours to know Jesus and his divine will. May I have no soul but yours to praise and glorify the Lord" (SM 68).

The following expression included in the prayer is especially relevant: *"I do not ask for visions or revelations, for sensible devotion or even spiritual pleasures"* (SM 69), recalling the *"pure faith"* that *"will cause you to depend less upon sensible and extraordinary feelings"* and of which we read in TD 214.

Finally, the triple Amen that concludes the prayer has no equivalent elsewhere in St. Louis de Montfort's work: *"The only grace I beg you in your kindness to obtain for me is that every day and moment of my life I may say this threefold Amen: Amen, so be it, to all you did upon earth; Amen, so be it, to all you are doing now in heaven; Amen, so be it, to all you are doing in my soul. In that way, you and you alone will fully glorify Jesus in me during all my life and my eternity"* (SM 69).

3. The cultivation and growth of the tree of life, in other words the way to make Mary live and reign in our souls

The expression *"Tree of Life,"* which Fr. de Montfort uses on a number of occasions in

his writings, does not always have the same application. In SM 22, it refers to the Cross of Jesus, and in Hymn 123:13, the Cross is Mary's Tree of Life. Elsewhere, as one finds in the majority of occurrences, for example, in SM 67, 78; TD 44, 164, 218, 261; *The Love of Eternal Wisdom* 204; and Hymn 81:7, Mary herself is the Tree of Life, and the fruit she bears is Jesus.

Saint Louis Marie begins by proclaiming the happiness of those who, thanks to the Holy Spirit, can have access to *"a secret of which very few people are aware. If you have discovered this treasure in the field of Mary, this pearl of great price, you should sell all you have to purchase it"* (SM 70). How highly Fr. de Montfort prizes his secret!

But what the Holy Spirit alone has planted must be cared for and cultivated: *"If the Holy Spirit has planted in your soul the true Tree of Life, which is the devotion that I have just explained, you should see carefully to its cultivation, so that it will yield its fruit in due season"* (SM 70).

How is it to be cultivated?

1. By counting on God alone:

"This tree, once planted in a docile heart,

requires fresh air and no human support. Being of heavenly origin, it must be uninfluenced by any creature, since a creature might hinder it from rising up towards God who created it. Hence you must not rely on your own endeavors or your natural talents or your personal standing or the guidance of men. You must resort to Mary, relying solely on her help" (SM 71).

Not that we are to wait passively for this tree to bear its fruit! Therefore:

2. By raising and tending the tree: "The person in whose soul this tree has taken root must, like a good gardener, watch over it and protect it. For this tree, having life and capable of producing the fruit of life, should be raised and tended with enduring care and attention of soul. A soul that desires to be holy will make this its chief aim and occupation" (SM 72).

The work of the gardener is to prune away anything that might hinder the growth of the tree. Accordingly, "by self-denial and self-discipline you must sedulously cut short and even give up all empty pleasures and useless dealings with other creatures. In other words, you must crucify the flesh, keep a guard over the tongue, and mortify the bodily senses" (SM 73).

3. *"You must guard against grubs doing harm to the tree. These parasites are love of self and love of comfort;... for love of self is incompatible with love of Mary"* (SM 74).

4. *"You must not allow this Tree to be damaged by destructive animals, that is, by sins."* And not only sins that deal death but even *"venial sins, which are most dangerous when we do not trouble ourselves about them"* (SM 75).

Over and above this struggle with what might assault the health of the tree, there is the whole positive aspect of a true spiritual life:

5. *"It is also necessary to water this Tree regularly with your Communions, Masses, and other public and private prayers. Otherwise it will not continue bearing fruit"* (SM 76).

6. Finally, we must not fear difficulties and contradictions, which are the lot of all who seek to follow Christ faithfully: *"This devotion to our Blessed Lady will surely be called into question and attacked. But as long as we continue steadfastly in tending [this tree], we have nothing to fear"* (SM 77).

Well protected and well cultivated, the Tree of Life will grow and *"will yield in due season the sweet and adorable Fruit of honor and grace, which is Jesus, who has always been and will always be the only fruit of Mary."* This enables Fr. de Montfort to conclude with the proclamation of a beatitude: *"Happy is the soul in which Mary, the tree of life, is planted. Happier still is the soul in which she has been able to grow and blossom. Happier again is the soul in which she brings forth her fruit. But happiest of all is the soul which savors the sweetness of Mary's fruit and preserves it up till death and then beyond to all eternity. Amen."* (SM 78).

THE SECRET
OF MARY

CONCERNING SLAVERY
TO THE HOLY VIRGIN

St. Louis de Montfort

THE SECRET OF MARY

1 Here is a secret[1], chosen soul, which the most High God taught me and which I have not found in any book, ancient or modern[2]. Inspired by the Holy Spirit, I am confiding it to you, with these conditions:

I. That you share it only with people who deserve to know it because they are prayerful, give alms to the poor, do penance, suffer persecution, are unworldly, and work seriously for the salvation of souls.

II. That you use this secret to become holy and worthy of heaven, for the more you make use of it the more benefit you will derive from it. Under no circumstances must you let this secret make you idle and inactive. It would then become harmful and lead to your ruin[3].

III. That you thank God every day of your life for the grace he has given you in letting you into a secret that you do not deserve to know.

As you go on using this secret in the ordinary actions of your life, you will come to understand its value and its excellent quality. At the beginning, however, your understanding of it will be clouded because of the seriousness and number

[1] Frequently in his writings Montfort speaks of a "secret." In SM 20 and TD 11, 248, 264, he uses the term in referring to the knowledge of Mary and the marvels of grace operated in her by God. Elsewhere "secret" is applied by him to the knowledge and practice of a marvellous means of acquiring holiness.

We may say that in Montfort's mind the term "secret" should be understood as meaning:

1. that the place and function of Mary in the saving work of God have not been sufficiently understood or inserted into the reality of the Christian life; 2. that we need a special grace from God to "understand and relish" (No. 2) the nature of this Marian devotion which enables us in our spiritual life to respond as perfectly as possible to the divine plan of salvation; 3. that this special Marian way of life does not just consist in a number of practices but in a disposition of the soul producing interior acts which constitute its essential element and are a rich source of grace.

[2] Montfort writes in LEW 219, TD 118, 159, and SM 42 that he had read almost all the books on the

subject of devotion to Mary and had never found a form of devotion to her like the one he is proposing. This devotion, he states, goes so far back into the history of the Church that it is impossible to see where it began (cf. TD 159, SM 42).

Cf. PIUS XII: Discourse of the pilgrims gathered for the Canonisation of St. Louis Marie de Montfort, 21 July 1947: "He attracted the enlightenment of God more by his life of prayer than by his active work. It was by this interior guidance that he understood and explained in his unique way what he found in the deposit of Revelation and in the Church's traditional devotion."

[3] This "caution" recalls the parable of the talents.

of your sins, and your unconscious love of self.

2 Before you read any further, in an understandable impatience to learn this truth, kneel down and say devoutly the *Ave Maris Stella* ("Hail, O Star of the Ocean"), and the *Veni, Creator* ("Come, Creator Spirit"), to ask God to help you understand and appreciate this secret given by him. As I have not much time for writing and you have little time for reading, I will be brief in what I have to say.

*Before continuing please turn to Appendix 1 (page 50) and devoutly pray these two prayers as recommended by Fr. de Montfort.

1. NECESSITY OF HAVING A TRUE DEVOTION TO MARY

A. THE GRACE OF GOD IS ABSOLUTELY NECESSARY

3 Chosen soul, living image of God and redeemed by the precious blood of Jesus Christ, God wants you to become holy like him in this life, and glorious like him in the next[4].

It is certain that growth in the holiness of God is your vocation. All your thoughts, words, actions, everything you suffer or undertake must lead you towards that end. Otherwise you are resisting God in not doing the work for which he created you and for which he is even now keeping you in being. What a marvellous transformation is possible! Dust into light, uncleanness into purity, sinfulness into holiness, creature into Creator, man into God! A marvellous work, I repeat, so difficult in itself, and even impossible for a mere creature to bring about, for only God can accomplish it by giving his grace abundantly and in an extraordinary manner. The very creation of the universe is not as great an achievement as this.

[4] Cf. Mt. 5:48.

[5] Montfort enlarges upon these means in other places, for example, Humility of heart: TD 143, 144; Continual prayer: LEW 184-193; Universal mortification: LEW 194-202; Abandonment to Providence: ACM 3-4; Conformity to the will of God: FC 51-53.

[6] Cf. Rom. 12:6.

4 Chosen soul, how will you bring this about? What steps will you take to reach the high level to which God is calling you? The means of holiness and salvation are known to everybody, since they are found in the gospel; the masters of the spiritual life have explained them; the saints have practiced them and shown how essential they are for those who wish to be saved and attain perfection. These means are: sincere humility, unceasing prayer, complete self-denial, abandonment to divine Providence, and obedience to the will of God[5].

5 The grace and help of God are absolutely necessary for us to practice all these, but we are sure that grace will be given to all, though not in the same measure. I say "not in the same measure", because God does not give his graces in equal measure to everyone[6], although in his infinite goodness he always gives sufficient grace to each. A person who corresponds to great graces performs great works, and one who corresponds to lesser graces performs lesser works. The value and high standard of our actions corresponds to the value and perfection of the grace given by God and responded to by the faithful soul. No one can contest these principles.

B. TO FIND THE GRACE OF GOD, WE MUST DISCOVER MARY

6 It all comes to this, then. We must discover a simple means to obtain from God the grace needed to become holy. It is precisely this I wish to teach you. My contention is that you must first discover Mary if you would obtain this grace from God.

7 Let me explain:
I. Mary alone found grace with God for herself and for every individual person[7]. No patriarch or prophet or any other holy person of the Old Law could manage to find this grace.

8 II. It was Mary who gave existence and life to the author of all grace, and because of this she is called the "Mother of Grace"[8].

9 III. God the Father, from whom, as from its essential source, every perfect gift and every grace come down to us[9], gave her every grace when he gave her his Son. Thus, as St. Bernard says, the will of God is manifested to her in Jesus and with Jesus[10].

[7] Cf. Lk. 1:30; SAINT BERNARD, On the Annunciation, sermon 3.

[8] This is a Marian title found frequently in spiritual authors. Montfort's text evokes the ideas expressed in Lumen Gentium No 61: Mary's unique cooperation "in the Saviour's work for the restoration of supernatural life to souls...This is the reason why she has been our Mother in the order of grace."

[9] Cf. Jas. 1:17.

[10] Cf. TD 25,141.

[11] Cf. TD 25.

[12] This whole number is a résumé of TD 23-25.

[13] Cf. TD 30.

[14] Cf. TD 32.

[15] Cf. Jn. 1:14.

10 **IV.** God chose her to be the treasurer, the administrator and the dispenser of all his graces, so that all his graces and gifts pass through her hands. Such is the power that she has received from him that, according to St. Bernardine[11], she gives the graces of the eternal Father, the virtues of Jesus Christ, and the gifts of the Holy Spirit to whom she wills, as and when she wills, and as much as she wills[12].

11 **V.** As in the natural life a child must have a father and a mother, so in the supernatural life of grace a true child of the Church must have God for his Father and Mary for his mother. If he prides himself on having God for his Father but does not give to Mary the tender affection of a true child, he is an impostor and his father is the devil[13].

12 **VI.** Since Mary produced the head of the elect, Jesus Christ, she must also produce the members of that head, that is, all true Christians. A mother does not conceive a head without members, nor members without a head[14]. If anyone, then, wishes to become a member of Jesus Christ, and consequently be filled with grace and truth[15], he must be formed

in Mary through the grace of Jesus Christ, which she possesses with a fullness enabling her to communicate it abundantly to true members of Jesus Christ, her true children.

13 **VII.** The Holy Spirit espoused Mary[16] and produced his greatest work, the incarnate Word, in her, by her and through her. He has never disowned her and so he continues to produce every day, in a mysterious but very real manner, the souls of the elect in her and through her[17].

14 **VIII.** Mary received from God a unique dominion over souls enabling her to nourish them and make them more and more godlike[18]. St. Augustine[19] went so far as to say that even in this world all the elect are enclosed in the womb of Mary, and that their real birthday is when this good mother brings them forth to eternal life. Consequently, just as an infant draws all its nourishment from its mother, who gives according to its needs, so the elect draw their spiritual nourishment and all their strength from Mary.

[16] Cf. TD 4.

[17] This whole number is a résumé of TD 34-36.

[18] Cf. TD 37.

[19] Cf. TD 33.

20 These three quotations are taken from Sir. 24:8, 12, and a fuller commentary is given in TD 29, 31.

21 Mary can be said to be present in us 1) by seeing and knowing us in the beatific vision; 2) by her influence as our spiritual Mother; 3) by our mystical union with her by love.

22 Attributed to St. Augustine but the true author of the sermon where it appears is Ambroise Autpert.

15 **IX.** It was to Mary that God the Father said, "Dwell in Jacob"[20], that is, dwell in my elect who are typified by Jacob. It was to Mary that God the Son said, "My dear Mother, your inheritance is in Israel", that is, in the elect. It was to Mary that the Holy Spirit said, "Place your roots in my elect". Whoever, then, is of the chosen and predestinate will have the Blessed Virgin living within him, and he will let her plant in his very soul[21] the roots of every virtue, but especially deep humility and ardent charity.

16 **X.** Mary is called by St. Augustine, and is indeed, the "living mould of God"[22]. In her alone the God-man was formed in his human nature without losing any feature of the Godhead. In her alone, by the grace of Jesus Christ, man is made godlike as far as human nature is capable of it.

A sculptor can make a statue or a life-like model in two ways: I. By using his skill, strength, experience and good tools to produce a statue out of hard, shapeless matter; II. By making a cast of it in a mould. The first way is long and involved and open to all sorts of accidents. It only needs a faulty stroke of the chisel or hammer to ruin the whole work. The second is quick, easy,

straightforward, almost effortless and inexpensive, but the mould must be perfect and true to life and the material must be easy to handle and offer no resistance.

17 Mary is the great mould of God, fashioned by the Holy Spirit to give human nature to a Man who is God by the hypostatic union, and to fashion through grace men who are like to God. No godly feature is missing from this mould. Everyone who casts himself into it and allows himself to be moulded will acquire every feature of Jesus Christ, true God, with little pain or effort, as befits his weak human condition. He will take on a faithful likeness to Jesus with no possibility of distortion, for the devil has never had and never will have any access to Mary, the holy and immaculate Virgin, in whom there is not the least suspicion of a stain of sin.

18 Dear friend, what a difference there is between a soul brought up in the ordinary way to resemble Jesus Christ by people who, like sculptors, rely on their own skill and industry, and a soul thoroughly tractable, entirely detached, most ready to be moulded in her by the working of the Holy Spirit. What blemishes and defects,

[23] This expression is unique in the works of Montfort. Generally he uses the phrase "Paradise of the new Adam" (cf. TD 6, Note 9).

[24] Is. 6:3.

what shadows and distortions, what natural and human imperfections are found in the first soul, and what a faithful and divine likeness to Jesus is found in the second!

19 There is not and there will never be, either in God's creation or in his mind, a creature in whom he is so honored as in the most Blessed Virgin Mary, not excepting even the saints, the cherubim or the highest seraphim in heaven.

Mary is God's garden of Paradise[23], his own unspeakable world, into which his Son entered to do wonderful things, to tend it and to take his delight in it. He created a world for the wayfarer, that is, the one we are living in. He created a second world - Paradise - for the Blessed. He created a third for himself, which he named Mary. She is a world unknown to most mortals here on earth. Even the angels and saints in heaven find her incomprehensible, and are lost in admiration of a God who is so exalted and so far above them, so distant from them, and so enclosed in Mary, his chosen world, that they exclaim: "Holy, holy, holy" unceasingly[24].

20 Happy, indeed sublimely happy, is the person to whom the Holy Spirit reveals the secret[25] of Mary, thus imparting to him true knowledge of her. Happy the person to whom the Holy Spirit opens this enclosed garden[26] for him to enter, and to whom the Holy Spirit gives access to this sealed fountain where he can draw water and drink deep draughts of the living waters of grace. That person will find only grace and no creature in the most lovable Virgin Mary. But he will find that the infinitely holy and exalted God is at the same time infinitely solicitous for him and understands his weaknesses. Since God is everywhere, he can be found everywhere, even in hell. But there is no place where God can be more present to his creature and more sympathetic to human weakness than in Mary. It was indeed for this very purpose that he came down from heaven. Everywhere else he is the Bread of the strong and the Bread of angels, but living in Mary he is the Bread of children[27].

21 Let us not imagine, then, as some misguided teachers do, that Mary being simply a creature would be a hindrance to union with the Creator[28]. Far from it, for it is no longer Mary who lives but Jesus Christ himself, God

[25] SM 1, Note 1.

[26] Song 4:12; TD 263, Note

[27] Cf. LEW 190; TD 208.

[28] Cf. TD 164-165.

[29] Cf. Gal. 2:20.

[30] Cf. TD 225.

[31] Cf. Lk. 1:45.

[32] Cf. TD 86.

alone, who lives in her. Her transformation into God far surpasses that experienced by St. Paul[29] and other saints, more than heaven surpasses the earth.

Mary was created only for God, and it is unthinkable that she should reserve even one soul for herself. On the contrary she leads every soul to God and to union with him. Mary is the wonderful echo of God[30]. The more a person joins himself to her, the more effectively she unites him to God. When we say "Mary", she re-echoes "God".

When, like St. Elizabeth, we call her blessed[31], she gives the honor to God. If those misguided ones who were so sadly led astray by the devil, even in their prayer-life, had known how to discover Mary, and Jesus through her, and God through Jesus[32], they would not have had such terrible falls. The saints tell us that when we have once found Mary, and through Mary Jesus, and through Jesus God the Father, then we have discovered every good. When we say "every good", we except nothing. "Every good" includes every grace, continuous friendship with God, every protection against the enemies of God, possession of truth to counter every falsehood, endless benefits and unfailing headway against the hazards we meet on the way to salvation, and finally every consolation and joy amid the bitter afflictions of life.

22 This does not mean that one who has discovered Mary through a genuine devotion is exempt from crosses and sufferings[33]. Far from it! One is tried even more than others, because Mary, as Mother of the living, gives to all her children splinters of the tree of life, which is the Cross of Jesus[34]. But while meting out crosses to them she gives the grace to bear them with patience, and even with joy. In this way, the crosses she sends to those who trust themselves to her are rather like sweetmeats, i.e. "sweetened" crosses rather than "bitter" ones. If from time to time they do taste the bitterness of the chalice from which we must drink to become proven friends of God, the consolation and joy which their Mother sends in the wake of their sorrows creates in them a strong desire to carry even heavier and still more bitter crosses.

[33] Cf. TD 153-154.

[34] Cf. SM 70. Note 97

[35] This is a difficult text. Montfort is certainly teaching the universality of the mediation of Mary in the distribution of graces according to God's plan. This teaching must be placed alongside the teaching of Vatican II, Lumen Gentium No. 60: "In the words of the Apostle our Mediator is unique. There is only one God and only one mediator between God and man, Christ Jesus… (1 Tim. 2:5). Mary's function as Mother of men makes for no dimming or diminution of this unique mediation of Christ but rather demonstrates his power. All the Blessed Virgin's salutary influence on men has its origin not in real necessity but in the divine decision; his mediation is its support, it is wholly dependent on that mediation, draws all its strength from it." Later in No. 62 the document makes a more general statement: "The unique mediation of the Redeemer does not exclude but rather stimulates among creatures a participation and cooperation which is varied but which originates from a single source."

The interpretation of this text can be reduced to three simple questions:

1. What is the order established by God in communicating himself to men? Montfort answers by saying that in the order of grace divine Wisdom does this ordinarily through Mary.

2. Absolutely speaking, can God communicate himself directly to men? Montfort answers, Yes, since God as the absolute Master can give to men directly what he ordinarily gives through Mary.

3. Does it actually happen that God gives graces directly to men independently of Mary? Montfort says it would be rash to say No.

C. A TRUE DEVOTION TO THE BLESSED VIRGIN IS INDISPENSABLE

23 The difficulty, then, is how to arrive at the true knowledge of the most holy Virgin and so find grace in abundance through her. God, as the absolute Master, can give directly what he ordinarily dispenses only through Mary, and it would be rash to deny that he sometimes does so. However, St. Thomas[35] assures us that, following the order established by his divine Wisdom, God ordinarily imparts his graces to men through Mary. Therefore, if we wish to go to him, seeking union with him, we must use the same means which he used in coming down from heaven to assume our human nature and to impart his graces to us. That means was a complete dependence on Mary his Mother, which is true devotion to her.

II. WHAT PERFECT DEVOTION TO MARY CONSISTS IN

A. SOME TRUE DEVOTIONS TO THE BLESSED VIRGIN MARY

24 There are indeed several true devotions to our Lady. I do not intend treating of those which are false[36].

25 The first[37] consists in fulfilling the duties of our Christian state, avoiding all mortal sin, performing our actions for God more through love than through fear, praying to our Lady occasionally, and honoring her as the Mother of God, but without our devotion to her being exceptional.

26 The second consists in entertaining for our Lady deeper feelings of esteem and love, of confidence and veneration. This devotion inspires us to join the confraternities of the Holy Rosary and the Scapular, to say the five or fifteen decades of the Rosary, to venerate our Lady's pictures and shrines, to make her known to others, and to enrol in her sodalities. This de-

[36] Cf. TD 92, Note

[37] Compare these three numbers 25-27 with TD 99, 115-117.

[38] Cf. TD 257 where this order is given differently.

votion, in keeping us from sin, is good, holy and praiseworthy, but it is not as perfect as the third, nor as effective in detaching us from creatures, or in practising that self-denial necessary for union with Jesus Christ.

27 The third devotion to our Lady is one which is unknown to many and practiced by very few. This is the one I am about to present to you.

B. THE PERFECT PRACTICE OF DEVOTION TO MARY

1. What it consists in

28 Chosen soul, this devotion consists in surrendering oneself in the manner of a slave to Mary, and to Jesus through her, and then performing all our actions with Mary, in Mary, through Mary, and for Mary[38].

Let me explain this statement further.

29 We should choose a special feast-day on which to give ourselves. Then, willingly and lovingly and under no constraint, we consecrate and sacrifice to her unreservedly our body and soul. We give to her our material possessions, such as house, family, income, and even the inner possessions of our soul, namely, our merits, graces, virtues and atonements[39].

Notice that in this devotion we sacrifice to Jesus through Mary all that is most dear to us, that is, the right to dispose of ourselves, of the value of our prayers and alms, of our acts of self-denial and atonements. This is a sacrifice which no religious order[40] would require of its members. We leave everything to the free disposal of our Lady, for her to use as she wills for the greater glory of God, of which she alone is perfectly aware[41].

30 We leave to her the right to dispose of all the satisfactory and prayer value of our good deeds, so that, after having done so and without going so far as making a vow, we cease to be master over any good we do. Our Lady may use our good deeds either to bring relief or deliverance to a soul in purgatory, or perhaps to bring a change of heart to a poor sinner.

[39] Cf. TD 121.

[40] That is, Order or religious Congregation.

[41] Cf. TD 123-124, 136.

[42] Cf. TD 122, 132.

[43] Cf. TD 69, 71.

31 By this devotion we place our merits in the hands of our Lady, but only that she may preserve, increase and embellish them, since merit for increase of grace and glory cannot be handed over to any other person. But we give to her all our prayers and good works, inasmuch as they have intercessory and atonement value, for her to distribute and apply to whom she pleases. If, after having thus consecrated ourselves to our Lady, we wish to help a soul in purgatory, rescue a sinner, or assist a friend by a prayer, an alms, an act of self-denial or an act of self-sacrifice, we must humbly request it of our Lady, abiding always by her decision, which of course remains unknown to us. We can be fully convinced that the value of our actions, being dispensed by that same hand which God himself uses to distribute his gifts and graces to us, cannot fail to be applied for his greatest glory[42].

32 I have said that this devotion consists in adopting the status of a slave with regard to Mary. We must remember that there are three kinds of slavery[43].

There is, first, a slavery based on nature. All men, good and bad alike, are slaves of God in this sense.

The second is a slavery of compulsion. The devils and the damned are slaves of God in this second sense.

The third is a slavery of love and free choice. This is the kind chosen by one who consecrates himself to God through Mary, and this is the most perfect way for us human beings to give ourselves to God, our Creator.

33 Note that there is a vast difference between a servant and a slave. A servant claims wages for his services, but a slave can claim no reward. A servant is free to leave his employer when he likes and serves him only for a time, but a slave belongs to his master for life and has no right to leave him. A servant does not give his employer a right of life and death over him, but a slave is so totally committed that his master can put him to death without fearing any action by the law.

It is easy to see, then, that no dependence is so absolute as that of a person who is a slave by compulsion. Strictly speaking, no man should be dependent to this extent on anyone except his Creator. We therefore do not find this kind of slavery among Christians, but only among Muslims and pagans.

[44] Cf. TD 126. Montfort presents his consecration as a perfect renewal of baptismal vows.

[45] Cf. TD 135, ff., where Montfort treats at length of the motives which recommend this devotion.

[46] Cf. TD 139-140.

[47] Cf. TD 142, Note

34 But happy, very happy indeed, will the generous person be who, prompted by love, consecrates himself entirely to Jesus through Mary as their slave, after having shaken off by baptism the tyrannical slavery of the devil[44].

2. The excellence of this practice of devotion

35 I would need much more enlightenment from heaven to describe adequately the surpassing merit of this devotional practice[45]. I shall limit myself to these few remarks:

I. In giving ourselves to Jesus through Mary's hands, we imitate God the Father, who gave us his only Son through Mary, and who imparts his graces to us only through Mary[46]. Likewise we imitate God the Son, who by giving us his example for us to follow, inspires us to go to him using the same means he used in coming to us, that is, through Mary. Again, we imitate the Holy Spirit, who bestows his graces and gifts upon us through Mary. "Is it not fitting," remarks St. Bernard, "that grace should return to its author by the same channel that conveyed it to us?"[47]

36 **II.** In going to Jesus through Mary, we are really paying honor to our Lord, for we are showing that, because of our sins, we are unworthy to approach his infinite holiness directly on our own. We are showing that we need Mary, his holy Mother, to be our advocate and mediatrix with him who is our Mediator. We are going to Jesus as Mediator and Brother, and at the same time humbling ourselves before him who is our God and our Judge. In short, we are practising humility, something which always gladdens the heart of God[48].

37 **III.** Consecrating ourselves in this way to Jesus through Mary implies placing our good deeds in Mary's hands. Now, although these deeds may appear good to us, they are often defective, and not worthy to be considered and accepted by God, before whom even the stars lack brightness.

Let us pray, then, to our dear Mother and Queen that having accepted our poor present, she may purify it, sanctify it, beautify it, and so make it worthy of God[49]. Any good our soul could produce is of less value to God our Father, in winning his friendship and favor, than a worm-eaten apple would be in the sight of

[48] Cf. TD 83-86, 143

[49] This whole passage is developed in TD 146-150.

[50] The same example is given in TD 147.

[51] Cf. TD 149, Note 218

[52] TD 144, 216.

[53] In TD 183-212 Montfort gives a long commentary on the biblical figure of Rebecca and Jacob.

a king, when presented by a poor peasant to his royal master as payment for the rent of his farm. But what would the peasant do if he were wise and if he enjoyed the esteem of the queen? Would he not present his apple first to her, and would she not, out of kindness to the poor man and out of respect for the king, remove from the apple all that was maggoty and spoilt, place it on a golden dish, and surround it with flowers? Could the king then refuse the apple? Would he not accept it most willingly from the hands of his queen who showed such loving concern for that poor man?[50] "If you wish to present something to God, no matter how small it may be," says St. Bernard[51], "place it in the hands of Mary to ensure its certain acceptance."

38 Dear God, how everything we do comes to so very little! But let us adopt this devotion and place everything in Mary's hands. When we have given her all we possibly can, emptying ourselves completely to do her honor, she far surpasses our generosity and gives us very much for very little. She enriches us with her own merits and virtues. She places our gift on the golden dish of her charity[52] and clothes us, as Rebecca clothed Jacob[53], in the beautiful

garments of her first-born and only Son, Jesus Christ, which are his merits, and which are at her disposal. Thus, as her servants and slaves, stripping ourselves of everything to do her honor, we are clad by her in double garments[54] - namely, the garments, adornments, perfumes, merits and virtues of Jesus and Mary. These are imparted to the soul of the slave who has emptied himself and is resolved to remain in that state.

39 **IV.** Giving ourselves in this way to our Lady is a practice of charity towards our neighbor[55] of the highest possible degree, because in making ourselves over to Mary, we give her all that we hold most dear and we let her dispose of it as she wishes in favor of the living and the dead.[56]

40 **V.** In adopting this devotion, we put our graces, merits and virtues into safe keeping by making Mary the depositary of them.[57] It is as if we said to her, "See, my dear Mother, here is the good that I have done through the grace of your dear Son. I am not capable of keeping it, because of my weakness and inconstancy, and also because so many wicked enemies are assailing me day and night. Alas, every day we see ce-

[54] Prov. 31:21; cf. TD 206.

[55] Cf. TD 171-172.

[56] In TD 132, Montfort answers objections on this point.

[57] This number is a résumé of the 8th motive of TD 173-178.

[58] Cf. Ps. 19:7

[59] 1 Tim. 6:20; 2 Tim. 1:12.

[60] SAINT BERNARD, Hom. 2 super Missus est. Cf. TD 174.

dars of Lebanon fall into the mire, and eagles which had soared towards the sun become birds of darkness, a thousand of the just falling to the left and ten thousand to the right.[58] But, most powerful Queen, hold me fast lest I fall. Keep a guard on all my possessions lest I be robbed of them. I entrust all I have to you,[59] for I know well who you are, and that is why I confide myself entirely to you. You are faithful to God and man, and you will not suffer anything I entrust to you to perish. You are powerful, and nothing can harm you or rob you of anything you hold."

"When you follow Mary you will not go astray; when you pray to her, you will not despair; when your mind is on her, you will not wander; when she holds you up, you will not fall; when she protects you, you will have no fear; when she guides you, you will feel no fatigue; when she is on your side, you will arrive safely home" (Saint Bernard). And again, "She keeps her Son from striking us; she prevents the devil from harming us; she preserves virtue in us; she prevents our merits from being lost and our graces from receding." These words of St. Bernard[60] explain in substance all that I have said. Had I but this one motive to impel me to choose this devotion, namely, that of keeping me in the

grace of God and increasing that grace in me, my heart would burn with longing for it.

41 This devotion makes the soul truly free by imbuing it with the liberty of the children of God.[61] Since we lower ourselves willingly to a state of slavery out of love for Mary, our dear Mother, she out of gratitude opens wide our hearts enabling us to walk with giant strides in the way of God's commandments.[62] She delivers our souls from weariness, sadness and scruples. It was this devotion that our Lord taught to Mother Agnes de Langeac,[63] a religious who died in the odor of sanctity, as a sure way of being freed from the severe suffering and confusion of mind which afflicted her. "Make yourself," she said, "my Mother's slave and wear her little chain." She did so, and from that time onwards her troubles ceased.

42 To prove that this devotion is authoritatively sanctioned, we need only recall the bulls of the popes and the pastoral letters of bishops recommending it, as well as the indulgences accorded to it, the confraternities founded to promote it, and the examples of many saints and illustrious people who have practiced it. But I do not see any necessity to record them here.[64]

[61] Cf. Rom. 8:21. This motive is developed in TD 169-170, 215.

[62] Cf. Ps. 18:6.

[63] AGNES DE LANGEAC (1602-1634), Prioress of the Dominican Sisters of the community of St. Catherine of Langeac. Cf. TD 170.

[64] Cf. TD 159-163 where Montfort gives a quick historical survey of eminent people who have practiced this devotion over the centuries.

[65] The order of these acts is given differently in TD 257.

3. *The interior constituents of this consecration and its spirit*

43 I have already said that this devotion consists in performing all our actions with Mary, in Mary, through Mary, and for Mary.[65]

44 It is not enough to give ourselves just once as a slave to Jesus through Mary; nor is it enough to renew that consecration once a month or once a week. That alone would make it just a passing devotion and would not raise the soul to the level of holiness which it is capable of reaching. It is easy to enroll in a confraternity; easy to undertake this devotion, and say every day the few vocal prayers prescribed. The chief difficulty is to enter into its spirit, which requires an interior dependence on Mary, and effectively becoming her slave and the slave of Jesus through her. I have met many people who with admirable zeal have set about practising exteriorly this holy slavery of Jesus and Mary, but I have met only a few who have caught its interior spirit, and fewer still who have persevered in it.

ACT WITH MARY

45 I. The essential practice of this devotion is to perform all our actions with Mary. This means that we must take her as the accomplished model for all we have to do.[66]

46 Before undertaking anything, we must forget self and abandon our own views.[67] We must consider ourselves as a mere nothing before God, as being personally incapable of doing anything supernaturally worthwhile or anything conducive to our salvation. We must have habitual recourse to our Lady, becoming one with her and adopting her intentions, even though they are unknown to us. Through Mary we must adopt the intentions of Jesus. In other words, we must become an instrument in Mary's hands for her to act in us and do with us what she pleases, for the greater glory of her Son; and through Jesus for the greater glory of the Father. In this way, we pursue our interior life and make spiritual progress only in dependence on Mary.

[66] Cf. TD 260.

[67] Montfort gives here two very important preconditions: to renounce oneself and to give oneself to Mary. In SM we find them here in the formula "With." In the TD it is placed in the formula " Through," No. 259.

[68] In explaining this formula Montfort uses here, as in TD 261-264, a series of symbols signifying the activity of our Lady and the cooperation of the soul in a life of intimate union which goes as far as identification.

[69] Cf. Song 4:4.

[70] Cf. Mt. 5:15; Lk. 8:16; 11:33.

ACT IN MARY

47 **II.** We must always act in Mary,[68] that is to say, we must gradually acquire the habit of recollecting ourselves interiorly and so form within us an idea or a spiritual image of Mary. She must become, as it were, an Oratory for the soul where we offer up our prayers to God without fear of being ignored. She will be as a Tower of David[69] for us where we can seek safety from all our enemies. She will be a burning lamp[70] lighting up our inmost soul and inflaming us with love for God. She will be a sacred place of repose where we can contemplate God in her company. Finally Mary will be the only means we will use in going to God, and she will become our intercessor for everything we need. When we pray we will pray in Mary. When we receive Jesus in Holy Communion we will place him in Mary for him to take his delight in her. If we do anything at all, it will be in Mary, and in this way Mary will help us to forget self everywhere and in all things.

ACT THROUGH MARY

71 Cf. TD 258.

72 Cf. TD 265.

48 **III.** We must never go to our Lord except through Mary, using her intercession and good standing with him.[71] We must never be without her when praying to Jesus.

ACT FOR MARY

49 **IV.** We must perform all our actions for Mary,[72] which means that as slaves of this noble Queen we will work only for her, promoting her interests and her high renown, and making this the first aim in all our acts, while the glory of God will always be our final end. In everything we must renounce self-love because more often than not, without our being aware of it, selfishness sets itself up as the end of all we work for. We should often repeat from the depths of our heart: "Dear Mother, it is to please you that I go here or there, that I do this or that, that I suffer this pain or this injury."

50 Beware, chosen soul, of thinking that it is more perfect to direct your work and intention straight to Jesus or straight to God. Without Mary, your work and your intention will be of little value. But if you go to God through

Mary, your work will become Mary's work, and consequently will be most noble and most worthy of God.

51 Again, beware of doing violence to yourself, endeavouring to experience pleasure in your prayers and good deeds. Pray and act always with something of that pure faith which Mary showed when on earth, and which she will share with you as time goes on. Poor little slave, let your sovereign Queen enjoy the clear sight of God, the raptures, delights, satisfactions and riches of heaven. Content yourself with a pure faith, which is accompanied by repugnance, distractions, weariness and dryness. Let your prayer be: "To whatever Mary my Queen does in heaven, I say Amen, so be it." We cannot do better than this for the time being.

52 Should you not savor immediately the sweet presence of the Blessed Virgin within you, take great care not to torment yourself. For this is a grace not given to everyone, and even when God in his great mercy favors a soul with this grace, it remains none the less very easy to lose it, except when the soul has become permanently aware of it through the habit of rec-

ollection. But should this misfortune happen to you, go back calmly to your sovereign Queen[73] and make amends to her.

4. The effects that this devotion produces in a faithful soul

53 Experience will teach you much more about this devotion than I can tell you, but, if you remain faithful to the little I have taught you, you will acquire a great richness of grace that will surprise you and fill you with delight.

54 Let us set to work, then, dear soul, through perseverance in the living of this devotion, in order that Mary's soul may glorify the Lord in us and her spirit be within us to rejoice in God her Savior.[74] Let us not think that there was more glory and happiness in dwelling in Abraham's bosom - which is another name for Paradise[75] - than in dwelling in the bosom of Mary where God has set up his throne. (Abbot Guerric)

55 This devotion faithfully practiced produces countless happy effects in the

[73] Montfort speaks here of a very high degree of grace, not given to everybody.

[74] Cf. SAINT AMBROSE, Exposit. in Luc II, No. 26.

[75] Cf. Lk. 16:22-23.

[76] Montfort explains these effects in TD 213-225.

[77] Accommodation to Mary of Gal. 2:20.

soul.[76] The most important of them is that it establishes, even here on earth, Mary's life in the soul, so that it is no longer the soul that lives, but Mary who lives in it.[77] In a manner of speaking, Mary's soul becomes identified with the soul of her servant. Indeed when by an unspeakable but real grace Mary most holy becomes Queen of a soul, she works untold wonders in it. She is a great wonder-worker especially in the interior of souls. She works there in secret, unsuspected by the soul, as knowledge of it might destroy the beauty of her work.

56 As Mary is everywhere the fruitful Virgin, she produces in the depths of the soul where she dwells a purity of heart and body, a singleness of intention and purpose, and a fruitfulness in good works. Do not think, dear soul, that Mary, the most faithful of all God's creatures, who went as far as to give birth to a God-man, remains idle in a docile soul. She causes Jesus to live continuously in that soul and that soul to live in continuous union with Jesus. If Jesus is equally the fruit of Mary for each individual soul as for all souls in general, he is even more especially her fruit and her masterpiece in the soul where she is present.

57 To sum up, Mary becomes all things for the soul that wishes to serve Jesus Christ. She enlightens his mind with her pure faith. She deepens his heart with her humility. She enlarges and inflames his heart with her charity, makes it pure with her purity, makes it noble and great through her motherly care. But why dwell any longer on this? Experience alone will teach us the wonders wrought by Mary in the soul, wonders so great that the wise and the proud, and even a great number of devout people find it hard to credit them.

58 As it was through Mary that God came into the world the first time in a state of self-abasement and privation, may we not say that it will be again through Mary that he will come the second time? For does not the whole Church expect him to come and reign over all the earth and to judge the living and the dead? No one knows how and when this will come to pass, but we do know that God, whose thoughts are further from ours than heaven is from earth,[78] will come at a time and in a manner least expected, even by the most scholarly of men and those most versed in Holy Scripture, which gives no clear guidance on this subject.

[78] Reference to Is. 55:8, 9.

[79] Cf. TD 226-256.

59 We are given reason to believe that, towards the end of time and perhaps sooner than we expect, God will raise up great men filled with the Holy Spirit and imbued with the spirit of Mary. Through them Mary, Queen most powerful, will work great wonders in the world, destroying sin and setting up the kingdom of Jesus her Son upon the ruins of the corrupt kingdom of the world. These holy men will accomplish this by means of the devotion of which I only trace the main outlines and which suffers from my incompetence.

5. Exterior practices

60 Besides interior practices, which we have just mentioned, this devotion has certain exterior practices which must not be omitted or neglected.[79]

CONSECRATION AND ITS RENEWAL

61 The first is to choose a special feast-day to consecrate ourselves through Mary to Jesus, whose slaves we are making ourselves. This

is an occasion for receiving Holy Communion and spending the day in prayer. At least once a year on the same day, we should renew the act of consecration.[80]

[80] Cf. TD 227-231.

[81] Cf. TD 232.

[82] Cf. TD 159. Note 251

OFFERING OF A TRIBUTE IN SUB-MISSION TO THE BLESSED VIRGIN

62 The second is to give our Lady every year on that same day some little tribute[81] as a token of our servitude and dependence. This has always been the customary homage paid by slaves to their master. This tribute could consist of an act of self-denial or an alms, or a pilgrimage, or a few prayers. St. Peter Damian tells us that his brother, Blessed Marino,[82] used to give himself the discipline in public on the same day every year before the altar of our Lady. This kind of zeal is not required, nor would we counsel it. But what little we give to our Lady we should at least offer with a heart that is humble and grateful.

83 Cf. TD 243-248.

84 Cf. TD 234, 235. The Montfortian version of the "Little Crown" is given among the Morning and Night Prayers.

A SPECIAL CELEBRATION OF THE FEAST OF THE ANNUNCIATION

63 The third practice is to celebrate every year with special fervor the feast of the Annunciation of our Lord.[83] This is the distinctive feast of this devotion and was chosen so that we might honor and imitate that dependence which the eternal Word accepted on this day out of love for us.

THE SAYING OF THE LITTLE CROWN AND THE MAGNIFICAT

64 The fourth practice is to say every day, without the obligation of sin, the prayer entitled "The Little Crown of the Blessed Virgin", which comprises three Our Fathers and twelve Hail Marys,[84] and to say frequently the Magnificat, which is the only hymn composed by our Lady. In the Magnificat we thank God for favouring us in the past, and we beg further blessings from him in the future. One special time when we should not fail to say it is during thanksgiving after Holy Communion. A person so scholarly as Gerson informs us that our Lady herself used to recite it in thanksgiving after Holy Communion.

THE WEARING OF A LITTLE CHAIN

65 The fifth is the wearing of a small blessed chain either around the neck, on the arm, on the foot, or about the body.[85] Strictly speaking, this practice can be omitted without affecting the essential nature of the devotion, but just the same it would be wrong to despise or condemn it, and foolhardy to neglect it.

Here are the reasons for wearing this external sign:

I. It signifies that we are free from the baneful chains of original and actual sin which held us in bondage.

II. By it we show our esteem for the cords and bonds of love with which our Lord let himself be bound that we might be truly free.

III. As these bonds are bonds of love,[86] they remind us that we should do nothing except under the influence of love.

IV. Finally, wearing this chain recalls to us once more that we are dependent on Jesus and Mary as their slaves. Eminent people[87] who had become slaves of Jesus and Mary valued these little chains so much that they were unhappy at not being allowed to trail them publicly like the slaves of the Muslims.

[85] Concerning the little chains cf. TD 236-242.

[86] Hos. 11:4; cf. also TD 237, 241.

[87] In TD 242 Montfort quotes the examples of Fr. Vincent Caraffa and Mother Agnes of Jesus.

These chains of love are more valuable and more glorious than the necklaces of gold and precious stones worn by emperors, because they are the illustrious insignia of Jesus and Mary, and signify the bonds uniting us to them.

It should be noted that if the chains are not of silver, they should for convenience' sake at least be made of iron.

They should never be laid aside at any time, so that they may be with us even to the day of judgement. Great will be the joy, glory and triumph of the faithful slave on that day when, at the sound of the trumpet, his bones rise from the earth still bound by the chain of holy bondage, which to all appearance has not decayed. This thought alone should convince a devout slave never to take off his chain, however inconvenient it may be.

III. SUPPLEMENT

A. A PRAYER TO JESUS

66 Most loving Jesus, permit me to express my heartfelt gratitude to you for your kindness in giving me to your holy Mother through the devotion of holy bondage, and so making her my advocate to plead with your Majesty on my behalf, and make up for all that I lack through my inadequacy.

Alas, O Lord, I am so wretched that without my dear Mother I would certainly be lost. Yes, I always need Mary when I am approaching you. I need her to calm your indignation at the many offences I have committed every day. I need her to save me from the just sentence of eternal punishment I have deservedly incurred. I need her to turn to you, speak to you, pray to you, approach you and please you. I need her to help me save my soul and the souls of others. In a word, I need her so that I may always do your holy will and seek your greater glory in everything I do.

Would that I could publish throughout the whole world the mercy which you have shown

[88] Ps. 118:56, quoted also in TD 179.

[89] Cf. Jn. 19:27; TD 179, Note

[90] Cf. SM 70, Note

to me! Would that the whole world could know that without Mary I would now be doomed! If only I could offer adequate thanks for such a great benefit as Mary! She is within me.[88] What a precious possession and what a consolation for me! Should I not in return be all hers? If I were not , how ungrateful would I be! My dear Saviour, send me death rather than I should be guilty of such a lapse, for I would rather die than not belong to Mary.

Like St. John the Evangelist at the foot of the Cross,[89] I have taken her times without number as my total good and as often have I given myself to her. But if I have not done so as perfectly as you, dear Jesus, would wish, I now do so according to your desire. If you still see in my soul or body anything that does not belong to this noble Queen, please pluck it out and cast it far from me, because anything of mine which does not belong to Mary is unworthy of you.

67 Holy Spirit, grant me all these graces. Implant in my soul the tree of true life,[90] which is Mary. Foster it and cultivate it so that it grows and blossoms and brings forth the fruit of life in abundance. Holy Spirit, give me a great love and longing for Mary, your exalted spouse.

Give me a great trust in her maternal heart and a continuous access to her compassion, so that with her you may truly form Jesus, great and powerful, in me until I attain the fullness of his perfect age.[91] Amen.

B. PRAYER TO MARY
For her faithful slaves

68 Hail, Mary, most beloved daughter of the eternal Father; hail, Mary, most admirable mother of the Son; hail, Mary, most faithful spouse of the Holy Spirit; hail, Mary, Mother most dear, Lady most lovable, Queen most powerful! Hail, Mary, my joy, my glory, my heart and soul.[92] You are all mine through God's mercy, but I am all yours in justice. Yet I do not belong sufficiently to you, and so once again, as a slave who always belongs to his master, I give myself wholly to you, reserving nothing for myself or for others.

If you still see anything in me which is not given to you, please take it now. Make yourself completely owner of all my capabilities. Destroy in me everything that is displeasing to God. Uproot it and bring it to nothing. Implant in me all that you deem to be good; improve it and make

[91] Cf. TD 33 Note . This text (Eph. 4:13) is very dear to Montfort and is met frequently in his writings. Cf. Act of Consecration in LEW 223.

[92] This greeting to Mary recalls that of the final prayer of the "Little Crown" (Morning Prayer) and can be considered as a renewal of the act of Consecration.

[93] These two phrases should be understood in the sense given in SM 37.

[94] Cf. SM 51.

it increase in me.

May the light of your faith dispel the darkness of my mind. May your deep humility take the place of my pride. May your heavenly contemplation put an end to the distractions of my wandering imagination. May your continuous vision of God fill my memory with his presence. May the burning love of your heart inflame the coldness of mine. May your virtues take the place of my sins. May your merits be my adornment and make up for my unworthiness before God.[93] Finally, most dearly beloved Mother, grant, if it be possible, that I may have no other spirit but yours to know Jesus and his divine will. May I have no soul but yours to praise and glorify the Lord. May I have no heart but yours to love God purely and ardently as you love him.

69 I do not ask for visions or revelations, for sensible devotion or even spiritual pleasures.[94] It is your privilege to see God clearly in perpetual light. It is your privilege to savor the delights of heaven where nothing is without sweetness. It is your privilege to triumph gloriously in heaven at the right hand of your Son without further humiliation, and to command angels, men, and demons, without resistance on

their part. It is your privilege to dispose at your own choice of all the good gifts of God without any exception.

Such, most holy Mary, is the excellent portion which the Lord has given you, and which will never be taken from you,[95] and which gives me great joy. As for my portion here on earth, I wish only to have a share in yours, that is, to have simple faith without seeing or tasting, to suffer joyfully without the consolation of men, to die daily to myself without flinching, to work gallantly for you even until death without any self-interest, as the most worthless of your slaves. The only grace I beg you in your kindness to obtain for me is that every day and moment of my life I may say this threefold Amen: Amen, so be it, to all you did upon earth; Amen, so be it, to all you are doing now in heaven; Amen, so be it, to all you are doing in my soul. In that way, you and you alone will fully glorify Jesus in me during all my life and throughout eternity. Amen.

[95] Allusion made to Lk. 10:42.

IV. THE CARE AND GROWTH OF THE TREE OF LIFE

OR, IN OTHER WORDS,
HOW BEST TO CAUSE MARY TO LIVE AND REIGN IN OUR SOULS

A. THE HOLY SLAVERY OF LOVE. THE TREE OF LIFE.

70 Have you understood with the help of the Holy Spirit what I have tried to explain in the preceding pages? If so, be thankful to God. It is a secret of which very few people are aware. If you have discovered this treasure in the field of Mary, this pearl of great price,[96] you should sell all you have to purchase it. You must offer yourself to Mary, happily lose yourself in her, only to find God in her.

If the Holy Spirit has planted in your soul the true Tree of Life,[97] which is the devotion that I have just explained, you should see carefully to its cultivation, so that it will yield its fruit in due season. This devotion is like the mustard seed of the Gospel,[98] which is indeed the small-

[96] Allusion to Mt. 13:44-46.

[97] The expression "Tree of Life" was first spoken of in Genesis 2:9. Montfort used the term in SM 22 in reference to the Cross of Jesus. Here, however, and in LEW and TD he identifies it with perfect devotion to Mary and describes the way to cultivate it.

[98] Marian accommodation of Mk. 4:31.

est of all seeds, but nevertheless it grows into a big plant, shooting up so high that the birds of the air, that is, the elect, come and make their nest in its branches. They repose there, shaded from the heat of the sun, and safely hidden from beasts of prey.

B. HOW TO CULTIVATE IT

Here is the best way, chosen soul, to cultivate it:

71 **I.** This tree, once planted in a docile heart, requires fresh air and no human support. Being of heavenly origin, it must be uninfluenced by any creature, since a creature might hinder it from rising up towards God who created it. Hence you must not rely on your own endeavours or your natural talents or your personal standing or the guidance of men. You must resort to Mary, relying solely on her help.

72 **II.** The person in whose soul this tree has taken root must, like a good gardener, watch over it and protect it. For this tree, having life and capable of producing the fruit of life, should be raised and tended with enduring care and attention of soul. A soul that desires to be

holy will make this its chief aim and occupation.

73 Whatever is likely to choke the tree or in the course of time prevent its yielding fruit, such as thorns and thistles, must be cut away and rooted out. This means that by self-denial and self-discipline you must sedulously cut short and even give up all empty pleasures and useless dealings with other creatures. In other words, you must crucify the flesh, keep a guard over the tongue, and mortify the bodily senses.

74 III. You must guard against grubs doing harm to the tree. These parasites are love of self and love of comfort, and they eat away the green foliage of the Tree and frustrate the fair hope it offered of yielding good fruit; for love of self is incompatible with love of Mary.

75 IV. You must not allow this tree to be damaged by destructive animals, that is, by sins, for they may cause its death simply by their contact. They must not be allowed even to breathe upon the Tree, because their mere breath, that is, venial sins, which are most dangerous when we do not trouble ourselves about them.

76 **V.** It is also necessary to water this Tree regularly with your Communions, Masses and other public and private prayers. Otherwise it will not continue bearing fruit.

77 **VI.** Yet you need not be alarmed when the winds blow and shake this tree, for it must happen that the storm-winds of temptation will threaten to bring it down, and snow and frost tend to smother it. By this we mean that this devotion to our Blessed Lady will surely be called into question and attacked. But as long as we continue steadfastly in tending it, we have nothing to fear.

C. ITS LASTING FRUIT: JESUS CHRIST

78 Chosen soul, provided you thus carefully cultivate the Tree of Life, which has been freshly planted in your soul by the Holy Spirit, I can assure you that in a short time it will grow so tall that the birds of the air will make their home in it. It will become such a good tree that it will yield in due season the sweet and adorable Fruit of honor and grace, which is Jesus, who has always been and will always be the only fruit of Mary.

Happy is that soul in which Mary, the Tree of Life,[99] is planted. Happier still is the soul in which she has been able to grow and blossom. Happier again is the soul in which she brings forth her fruit. But happiest of all is the soul which savors the sweetness of Mary's fruit and preserves it up till death and then beyond to all eternity. Amen.

"Let him who possesses it, hold fast to it."[100]

[99] Cf. SM 70, Note

[100] These words seem to be inspired by 2 Thess. 2:7. The text of Montfort signifies: Let him who possesses this precious doctrine preserve it with care and faithfulness.

Appendix 1

Ave Maris Stella
(Hail, O Star of the Ocean)

(English)

HAIL, O Star of the ocean,
God's own Mother blest,
ever sinless Virgin,
gate of heavenly rest.

Taking that sweet Ave,
which from Gabriel came,
peace confirm within us,
changing Eve's name.

Break the sinners' fetters,
make our blindness day,
Chase all evils from us,
for all blessings pray.

Show thyself a Mother,
may the Word divine
born for us thine Infant
hear our prayers through thine.

Virgin all excelling,
mildest of the mild,
free from guilt preserve us
meek and undefiled.

(Latin)

AVE maris stella,
Dei Mater alma,
atque semper Virgo,
felix caeli porta.

Sumens illud Ave
Gabrielis ore,
funda nos in pace,
mutans Hevae nomen.

Solve vincula reis,
profer lumen caecis
mala nostra pelle,
bona cuncta posce.

Monstra te esse matrem:
sumat per te preces,
qui pro nobis natus,
tulit esse tuus.

Virgo singularis,
inter omnes mites,
nos culpis solutos,
mites fac et castos.

Keep our life all spotless,
make our way secure
till we find in Jesus,
joy for evermore.

Praise to God the Father,
honor to the Son,
in the Holy Spirit,
be the glory one.
Amen.

Vitam praesta puram,
iter para tutum:
ut videntes Iesum
semper collaetemur.

Sit laus Deo Patri,
summo Christo decus,
Spiritui Sancto,
tribus honor unus.
Amen.

VENI, CREATOR
(COME, CREATOR SPIRIT)

(ENGLISH)

COME, Holy Spirit, Creator blest,
and in our souls take up Thy rest;
come with Thy grace and heavenly aid
to fill the hearts which Thou hast made.

O comforter, to Thee we cry,
O heavenly gift of God Most High,
O fount of life and fire of love,
and sweet anointing from above.

Thou in Thy sevenfold gifts are known;
Thou, finger of God's hand we own;
Thou, promise of the Father, Thou
Who dost the tongue with power imbue.

Kindle our sense from above,
and make our hearts o'erflow with love;
with patience firm and virtue high
the weakness of our flesh supply.

Far from us drive the foe we dread,
and grant us Thy peace instead;
so shall we not, with Thee for guide,
turn from the path of life aside.

(LATIN)

VENI, Creator Spiritus,
mentes tuorum visita,
imple superna gratia
quae tu creasti pectora.

Qui diceris Paraclitus,
altissimi donum Dei,
fons vivus, ignis, caritas,
et spiritalis unctio.

Tu, septiformis munere,
digitus paternae dexterae,
Tu rite promissum Patris,
sermone ditans guttura.

Accende lumen sensibus:
infunde amorem cordibus:
infirma nostri corporis
virtute firmans perpeti.

Hostem repellas longius,
pacemque dones protinus:
ductore sic te praevio
vitemus omne noxium.

Oh, may Thy grace on us bestow
the Father and the Son to know; and
Thee, through endless times confessed,
of both the eternal Spirit blest.

Now to the Father and the Son,
Who rose from death, be glory given,
with Thou, O Holy Comforter,
henceforth by all in earth and heaven.

Amen.

Per te sciamus da Patrem,
noscamus atque Filium;
Teque utriusque Spiritum
credamus omni tempore.

Deo Patri sit gloria,
et Filio, qui a mortuis
surrexit, ac Paraclito,
in saeculorum saecula.

Amen.

APPENDIX II

From the collection of the Hymns of St. Louis Marie de Montfort. Translated into English by Fr. J. Patrick Gaffney, SMM.

HYMN 77:
THE DEVOUT SLAVE OF JESUS IN MARY

1. Sing out my soul! Make known
   To the glory of my Savior,
   Mary's great mercy
   Toward her poor servant.

2. Would that I had a voice of thunder
   To proclaim far and near:
   The happiest people on this earth
   Are those who serve her best.

3. Christians, open your ears!
   Listen to me, chosen souls!
   The marvels I shall now relate
   Of her who gave you birth.

4. MARY is my greatest fortune
   And my all at Jesus' throne.
   She is my tenderness and my honor,
   The treasure house of all my worth.

5. She is my Covenant Ark
   Where all holiness I find,
   She is my robe of innocence
   Concealing all I lack.

6. She is my divine oratory
   Where Jesus is always found,
   I pray there all times blissfully,
   Never fearing a rebuff.

7. She is my city of refuge
   Where I cannot be harmed.
   She is my ark in deluge;
   There, I shall never drown.

8. On her I am totally dependent,
   On my Savior more so to depend,
   Leaving everything to His care,
   My body, soul and all my joy.

9. When I rise to God my Father
   From the depths of my iniquity,
   On my Mother's wings I'm carried,
   Thanks to the goodness of her support.

10. To soothe Jesus in His anger,
    Comes so easy with Mary.
    I tell Him: "Behold your Mother"
    And He is calmed at once.

11. This kind Mother and Mistress
    Greatly helps me everywhere
    And when I fall through weakness
    She raises me up right away.

12. When my soul is troubled
    By my daily sins,
    It becomes unruffled,
    Saying: Mary, help!

13. She tells me in her own way
    When I am in a struggle:
    Courage, my child, courage,
    I shall not abandon you.

14. As a baby at the breast
    I am held so close to her.
    This pure and faithful Virgin
    Feeds me milk all divine.

15. Here is something hard to grasp:
    In my heart's center I carry her
    Etched with strokes of glory,
    Yet in faith's darkness still.

16. She makes me pure and fruitful
    By her pure fecundity,
    She makes me strong and docile
    By her deep humility.

17. Mary is my clear fountain
    Where I discover all my flaws,
    Where I delight so freely
    And temper all my passions.

18. I go through Jesus to his Father,
    Never am I rebuffed;
    I go to Jesus through his Mother.
    Never am I spurned.

19. I do everything in and by her,
    What a secret of holiness,
    Keeping me ever faithful
    To always do God's holy will.

20. Christians, provide, I implore,
    For my huge infidelity;
    Love Jesus, love Mary,
    In time and in eternity.
    GOD ALONE

THE MISSIONARIES OF THE COMPANY OF MARY
(Montfort Missionaries)
AD JESUM PER MARIAM

The spiritual legacy contained within the life and writings of St. Louis de Montfort is one of the truly great treasures of the Roman Catholic Church. The task of bringing the full wealth of that treasure to the faithful is the heart of the mission of the MISSIONARIES OF THE COMPANY OF MARY (Montfort Missionaries), the community of those priests and brothers who have been consecrated to follow in his footsteps. Since our foundation by St. Louis de Montfort, the missionary activity of the Company of Mary has grown to include active apostolates serving the needs of the people of God in nearly thirty countries.

MONTFORT PUBLICATIONS is a ministry of the Company of Mary through which we make available the writings of St. Louis de Montfort and resources to assist the faithful in understanding and living the full depth of his profound spirituality.

Montfort Publications | 631.665.0726
26 South Saxon Avenue | *info@montfortpublications.com*
Bay Shore, NY 11706 | *MontfortPublications.com*